July 2002

To: Mrs Lee

From: Julie Watson

Debbie & Jo's Mother
Femi's Friend

Prayers
in time of
Sorrow

Kevin
Mayhew

First published in Great Britain in 1993 by
KEVIN MAYHEW LTD
Rattlesden
Bury St Edmunds
Suffolk IP30 0SZ

Lutheran Publishing House
205 Halifax Street
Adelaide
SA 5000
Australia

ISBN 0 86209 422 4

Printed in Hong Kong
by Colorcraft

CONTENTS

4

TAKE COURAGE!

I can't change what you're going through,
I have no words to make a difference,
no answers or solutions
to make things easier for you.

But if it helps in any way
I want to say I care.

Please know that even when you're lonely
you're not alone.

I'll be here,
supporting you with all my thoughts,
cheering for you with all my strength,
praying for you with all my heart.

For whatever you need,
for as long as it takes –

Lean on my love.

You shall go out in joy,
and be led back in peace;
the mountains and the hills
before you
shall burst into song,
and all the trees of the field
shall clap their hands.
Instead of the thorn
shall come up the cypress;
instead of the brier
shall come up the myrtle;
and it shall be to the Lord
for a memorial,
for an everlasting sign
that shall not be cut off.

Isaiah 55:12-13

Earth has no sorrow
that heaven cannot heal.

Lord, you have been our dwelling place
in all generations.
Before the mountains were brought forth,
or you had formed the earth
and the world,
from everlasting to everlasting
you are God.

PSALM 90:1-2

My Peace I Give
Unto You

Blessed are the eyes that see
the things that you have seen,
blessed are the feet that walk
the ways where you have been.

Blessed are the eyes that see
the agony of God,
blessed are the feet that tread
the paths his feet have trod.

Blessed are the souls that solve
the paradox of pain,
and find the path that, piercing it,
leads through to peace again.

G. A. STUDDERT-KENNEDY

You are no stranger
to my heavy heart, Lord.
You take upon yourself
the grief I bear.

I find strength and hope, Lord,
in your promise
that where I am,
you also will be there.

I Am With You Always

In the springtime of your life,
when joy is new,
and when the summer brings the fullness
of your faith, I'm there with you.
I am with you in the autumn
of your years to turn to gold
every memory of your yesterdays,
to banish winter's cold.
I am with you in the sunshine,
when your world glows warm and bright.
I am with you when life's shadows
bring long hours of endless night.
I am with you every moment,
every hour of every day.
Go in peace upon life's journey,
for I'm with you all the way.

13

WHEN DREAMS ARE BROKEN

When dreams are broken things
and joy has fled,
there is Jesus.
When hope is a struggle
and faith a fragile thread,
there is Jesus.

When grief is a shadow
and peace unknown,
there is Jesus.
When we need the assurance
that we're not alone,
there is Jesus.

Be still, and know
that I am God.

PSALM 46:10

In sorrow and suffering,
go straight to God in confidence
and you will be strengthened,
enlightened and instructed.

In you, O Lord,
I seek refuge;
do not let me ever be put to shame;
in your righteousness deliver me.
Incline your ear to me;
rescue me speedily.
Be a rock of refuge for me,
a strong fortress to save me.
You are indeed my rock
and my fortress;
for your name's sake
lead me and guide me.

PSALM 31:1-3

Know that I am with you always:
yes, even to the end of time.

MATTHEW 28:20

17

WINGS OF FAITH

Give us, Lord, a special faith,
unlimited and free,
a faith that isn't bound
by what we know or what we see.

A faith that trusts the sunshine
even when there is no light,
a faith that hears the morning song's
soft echo in the night.

A faith that somehow rises
past unhappiness or pain,
knowing that in every loss
your goodness will remain.

A faith that finds your steadfast love
sufficient for all things,
a faith that lifts the heart above
and gives the spirit wings.

He comes, the Consolation of the suffering,
the Light that breaks through
darkness and despair.
He comes, and we discover that his presence
is the loving answer to our every prayer.

GOD HAS NOT PROMISED

God has not promised
sun without rain,
joy without sorrow,
peace without pain.
But God has promised
strength for the day,
rest for the labour,
light for the way,
grace for the trials,
help from above,
unfailing sympathy,
undying love.

Peace on the outside
comes from
knowing God within.

BEYOND THE SHADOWS

Let me look beyond the gathering shadows
of today, Lord.
Help me see tomorrow's hope,
even through my tears.
Shine your gentle sunlight on the winter
of my soul, Lord.
Warm my spirit with your love
until spring reappears.

The Lord will turn
the darkness before you
into light.

ISAIAH 42:16

Blessed are you when people hate you,
and when they exclude you,
revile you, and defame you
on account of the Son of Man.
Rejoice in that day and leap for joy,
for surely your reward is great in heaven;
for that is what their ancestors
did to the prophets.

LUKE 6:22-23

Peace I leave with you; my peace I give to you. I do not give to you as the world gives. Do not let your hearts be troubled, and do not let them be afraid.

JOHN 14:27

Be strong and courageous.
Do not be afraid or discouraged,
for I, the Lord your God,
am with you wherever you go.

Joshua 1:9

Do Not Be Afraid

Do not be afraid, for I have redeemed you.
I have called you by your name;
you are mine.

When you walk through the waters,
I'll be with you;
you will never sink beneath the waves.

When the fear of loneliness is looming,
then remember I am at your side.

You are mine, O my child, I am your Father,
and I love you with a perfect love.

Based on Isaiah 43:1-5

WHEN YOU'RE LONELY

When you're lonely,
I wish you love.

When you're down,
I wish you joy.

When you're troubled,
I wish you peace.

When things are complicated,
I wish you simple beauty.

When things look empty,
I wish you hope.

Lord, may we find peace in your love,
joy in your mercies
and strength in your touch.

Going a little farther,
he threw himself
on the ground and prayed,
'My Father, if it is possible,
let this cup pass from me;
yet not what I want
but what you want.'

MATTHEW 26:39

Rosa alba Regalis.   *Rosier blanc Royal.*

A BLESSING

May the Lord bless you
and take care of you;

May the Lord be kind
and gracious to you;

May the Lord look on you with favour
and give you peace.

NUMBERS 6:22-27

ACKNOWLEDGEMENTS

The publishers wish to express their gratitude to Fine Art Photographic Library, London, and the Galleries listed below, for permission to reproduce the pictures in this book:

Front Cover ROSES, 1882 by Alexandre Debrus.
Private Collection.

Page 4 CONSOLATION by Knut Ekwall (1843-1912).
Galerie George.

Page 7 THE ORCHARD AT BLOSSOM TIME by Juliette Wystman (1866-1925).
Galerie Berko.

Page 8 SWANS BY THE RIVERBANK by Valentine J. Davis (1854-1930).
By courtesy of P. Parker, Esq.

Pages 10 & 11 PRIMROSES by Sidney Shelton. Caelt Gallery.

Page 13 A FLOWERY GLADE by Alfred Parsons (1847-1920).
By courtesy of Mr Fulda.

Page 15 DAYDREAMING by Dewey Bates (1851-1899).
Anthony Mitchell Fine Paintings, Nottingham.

Page 16 A SPRING IDYLL by Charles H. Whitworth (fl. 1875-1915).
Hampshire Gallery.

Page 19 THE BUTTERFLIES' HAUNT by W. Scott Myles (19c).
Anthony Mitchell Fine Paintings, Nottingham.

Page 20 COTTAGES ON THE RIVER by Arthur Claude Strachan (1865-1954).
© control. By courtesy of Mr Fulda.

Page 23 WATERLILIES by William Jabez Muckley (1837-1905).
Cider House Gallery.

Pages 24 & 25 HAZY SUNSHINE (SUNSET) by Albert Gabriel Rigolot (1862-1932).
Eaton Gallery, London SW1.

Page 26 LAMBING TIME by Basil Bradley (1842-1904).
Bourne Gallery.

Page 29 THE SUN-DIAL by Ernest Albert Chadwick.
Private Collection.

Page 30 ROSA ALBA REGALIS by Pierre Joseph Redoute (1759-1840).